To help your child learn to write effectively, we recommend the following preparations:

1. Development of Postural Control

- It is important for your child to be able to keep their body balanced while in a sitting position (without using their hands to stabilize).

- When writing, ensure your child's back is straight, elbows and knees are bent at 90-degree angles, feet are flat on the floor or on the chair's footrest, and the paper or workbook is angled with the corner of the page pointing toward the child's torso.

- If you notice your child consistently sitting with poor posture—leaning on one arm or slouching—this is not a sign of laziness or a lack of motivation.

- Try incorporating one of these core exercises into your child's daily routine to help strengthen their postural chain: ride a bike, swim, jump, climb, crab-walk, do sit-ups, roll from their back to their belly in both directions, dance, swing, bounce on a trampoline, or play Red Light, Green Light.

2. Development of Tripod Grasp and Fine Motor Skills

- To hold a pencil, children need to practice grabbing and pinching objects daily to strengthen the small muscles in their hands and wrists.

- Let them experience a wide range of activities to build these muscles, such as playing with building blocks, clay, puzzles, or origami.

- Research shows that if we engage fine motor muscles in a multisensory way, kids will develop writing skills much earlier and will have more fun while writing! Try the following activities: drawing in salt, dirt, cinnamon, sand, flour; picking up pom-poms with tweezers; using a hole punch; taking stickers off a sticker sheet and sticking them on a piece of paper; and playing with clothespins.

- If you don't have enough time to practice with your child, you can incorporate fine motor activities into your daily routine, such as allowing your child to pick up and put cereal in their own mouth or helping them learn to pick up and put blocks away when it is time to clean up.

3. Keep It Fun

- Make writing feel like play! For example, while using this book, you could ask your child to pretend that the pencil tip is a race car that cannot go off the dotted-line track—otherwise, it will crash.

- If your child starts to scribble or do something silly, this is a sign that they are feeling uncomfortable or nervous about proceeding. Give some gentle encouragement and ask them if they would like a blank sheet of paper to make a drawing instead. Scribbling is just as important to writing development as letter tracing.

- Remember, writing is HARD. Many different systems of the brain and body must work together for children to learn to write properly. Children need visual perception, visual memory, spatial awareness, sensory processing, executive functioning skills, and self-regulation, as well as fine motor skills, bilateral coordination between both sides of the body, and a strong core and attention span to be successful writers.

Happy writing!

Katerina A. Walls, Cognitive Development Specialist

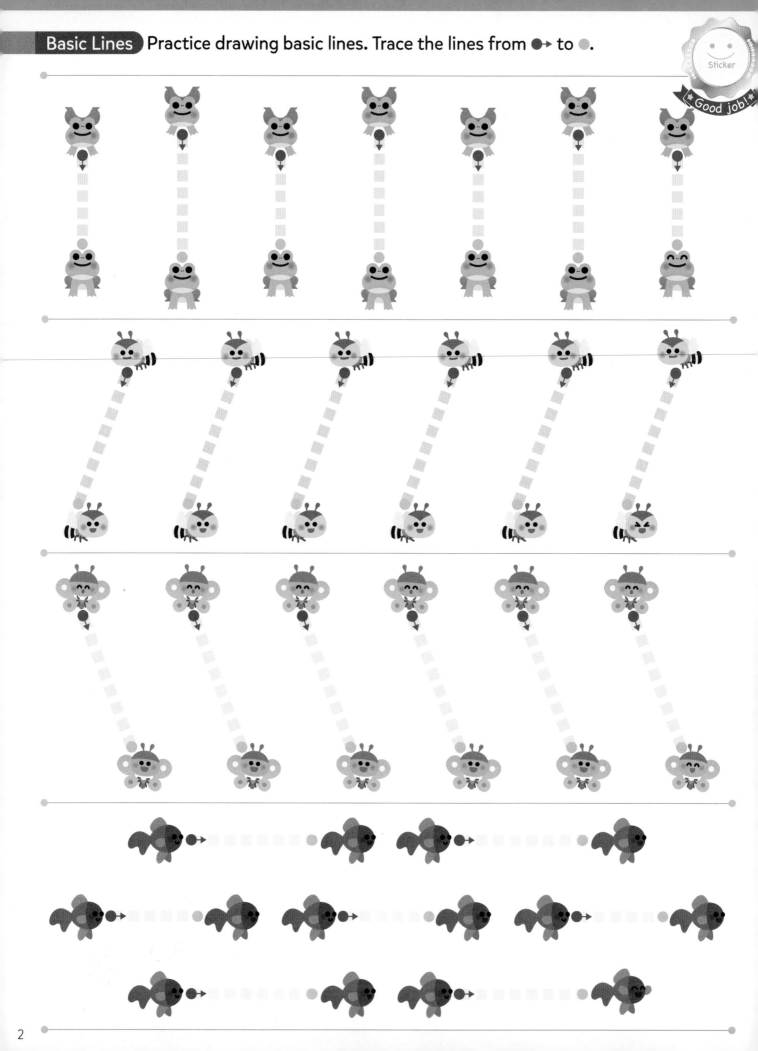

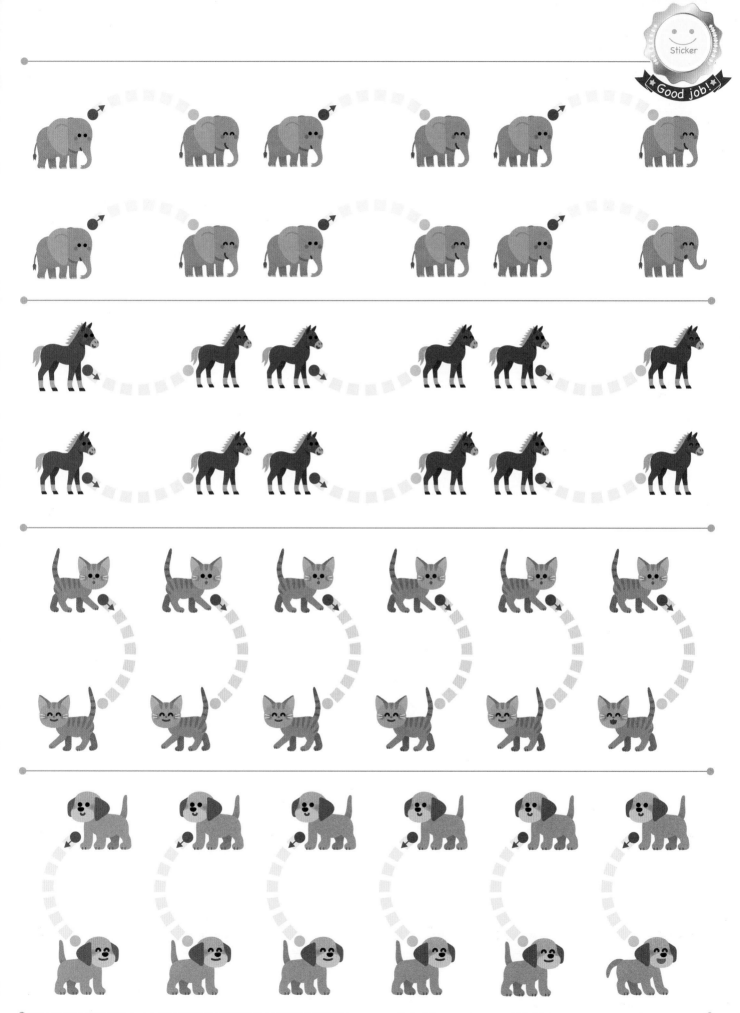

Sticker

Good job!

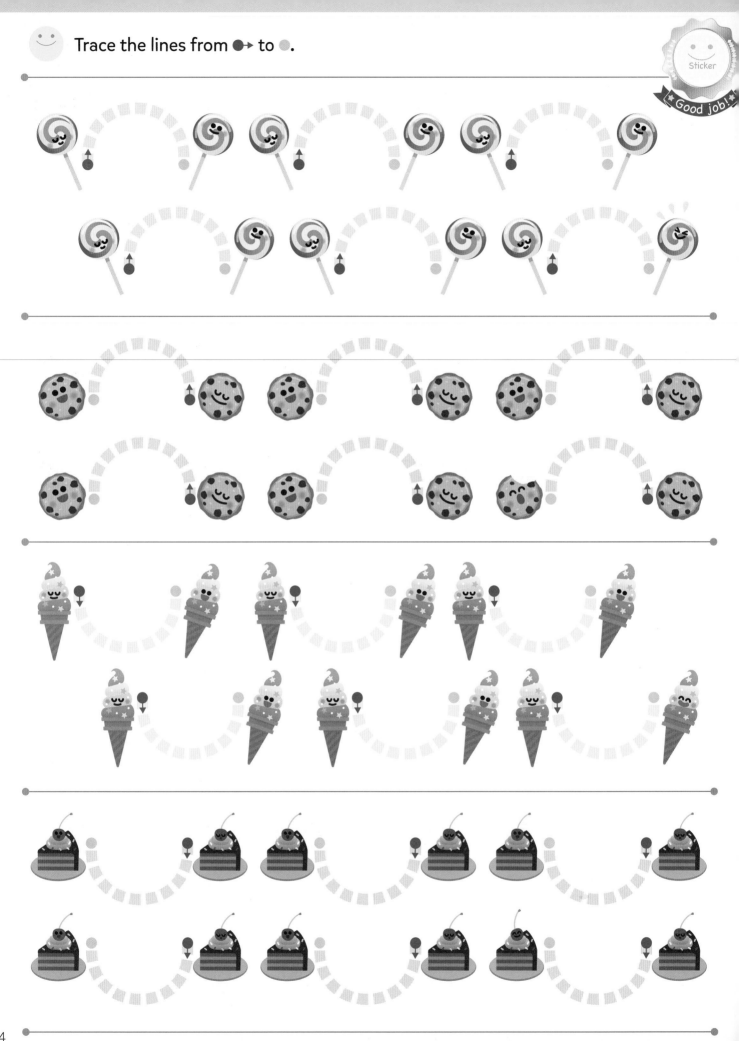

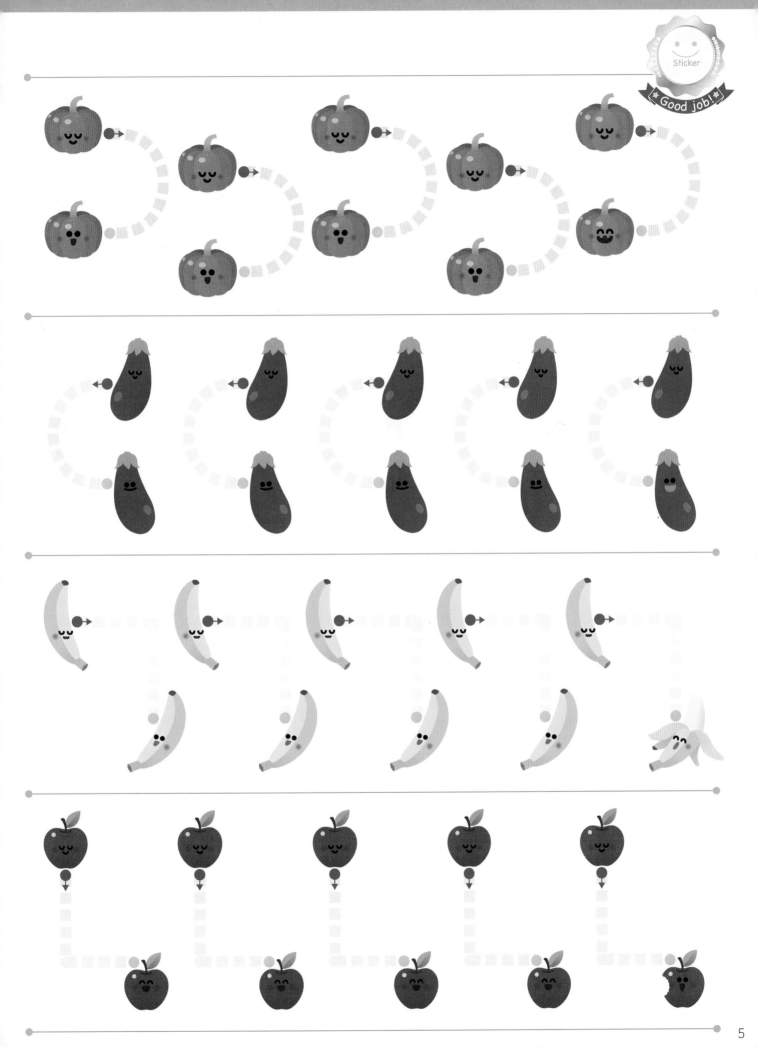

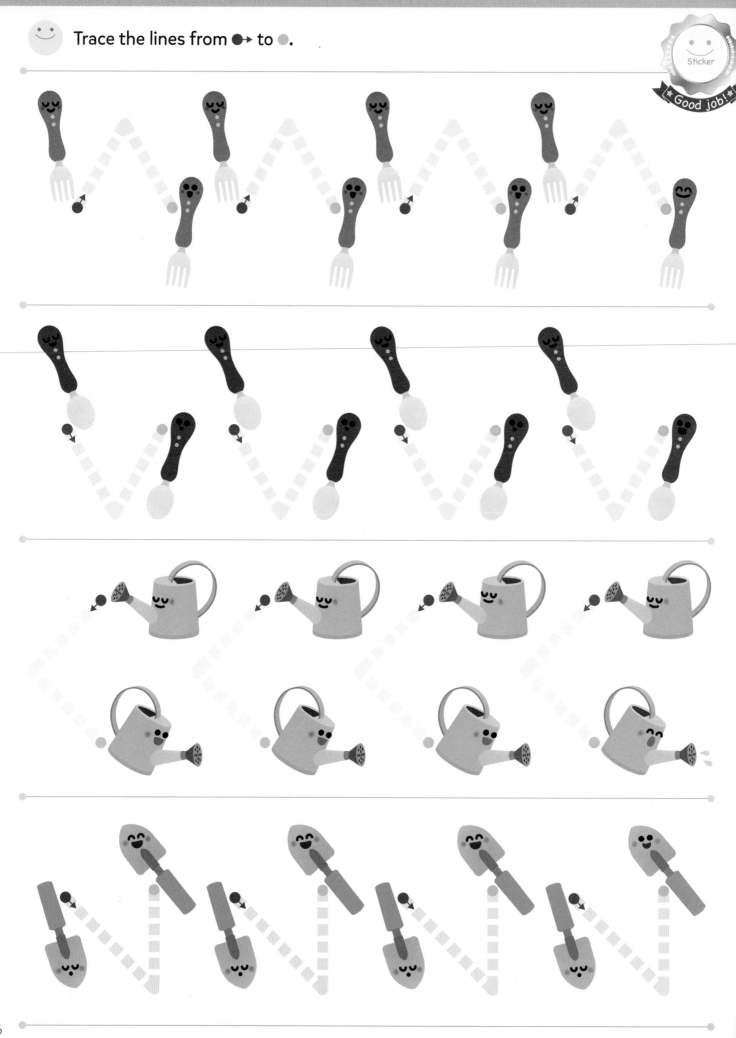

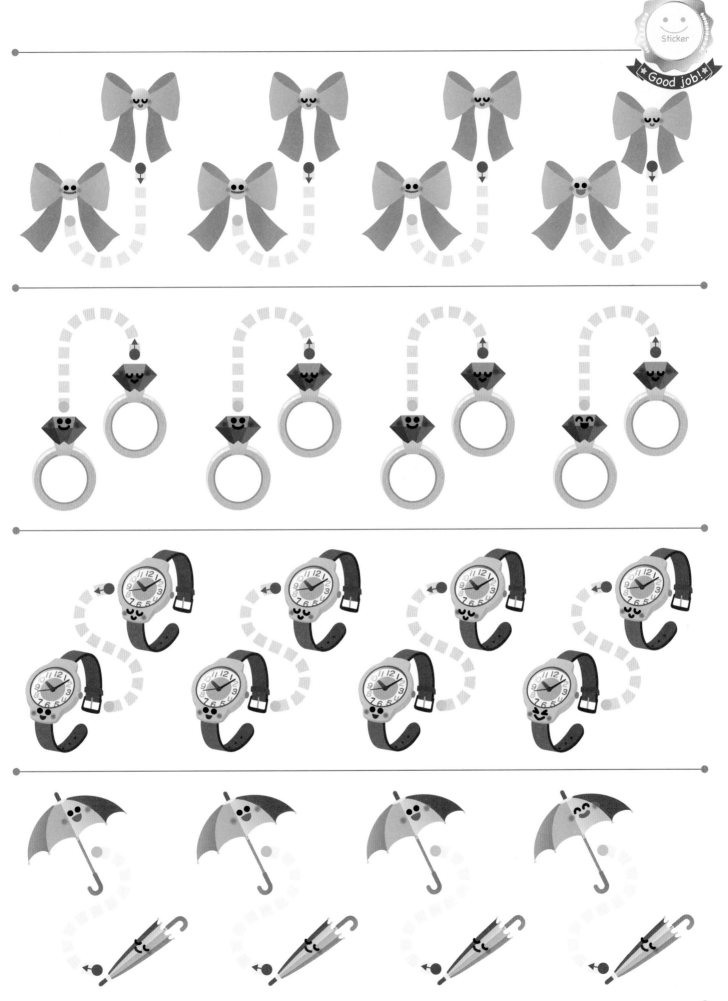

Trace the lines from ● to ●.

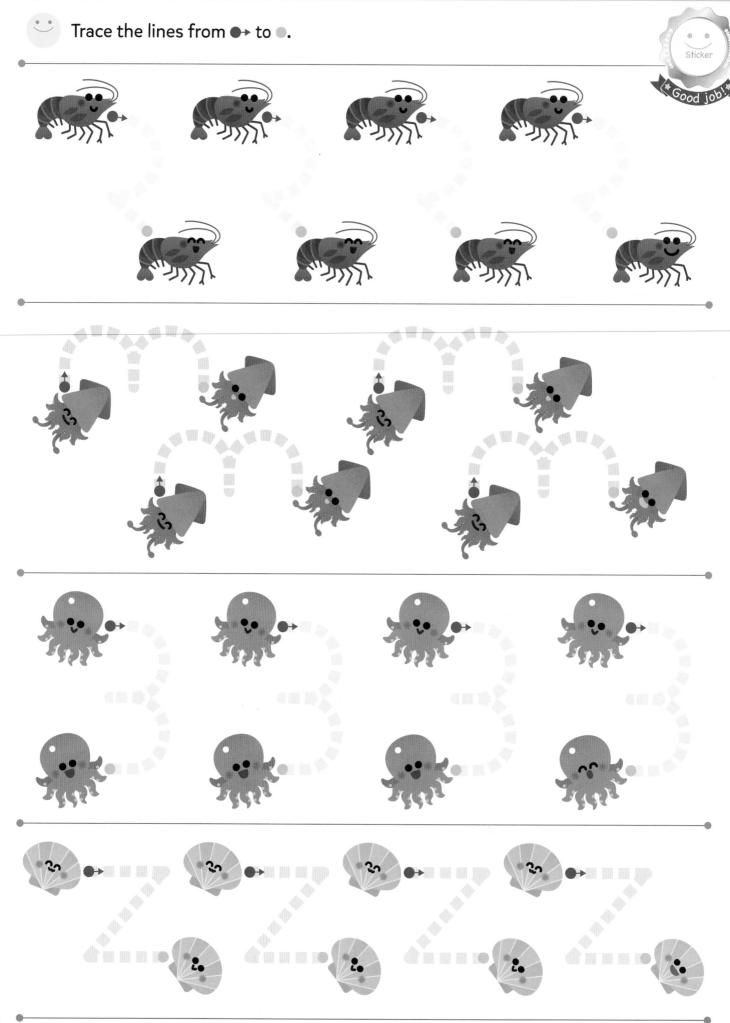

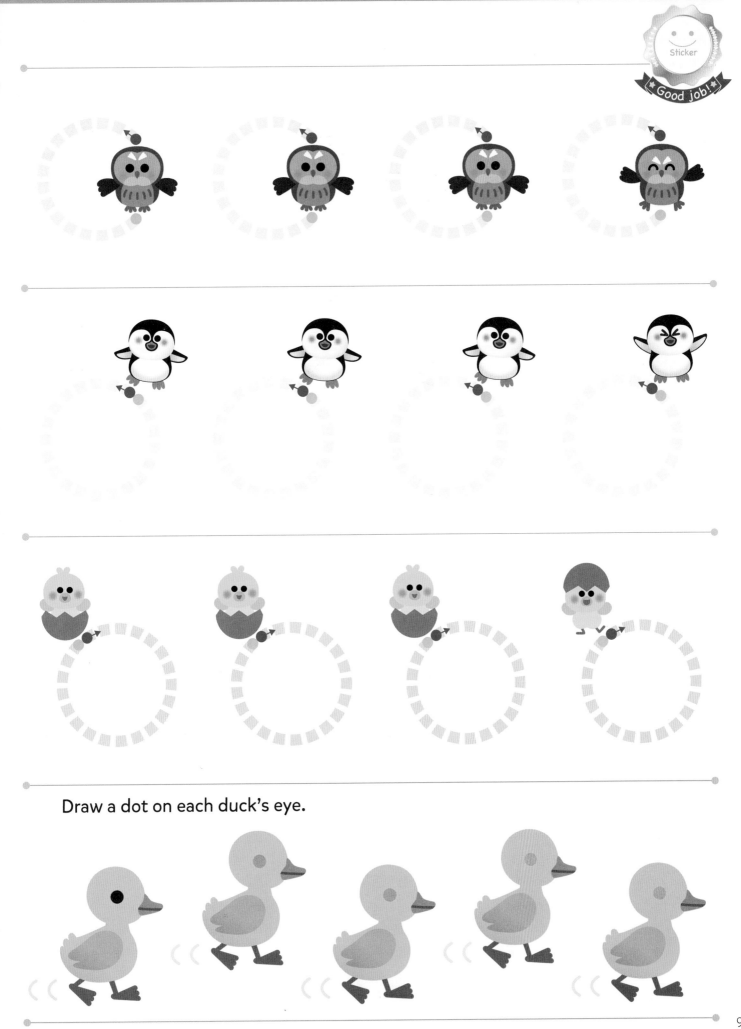

Draw a dot on each duck's eye.

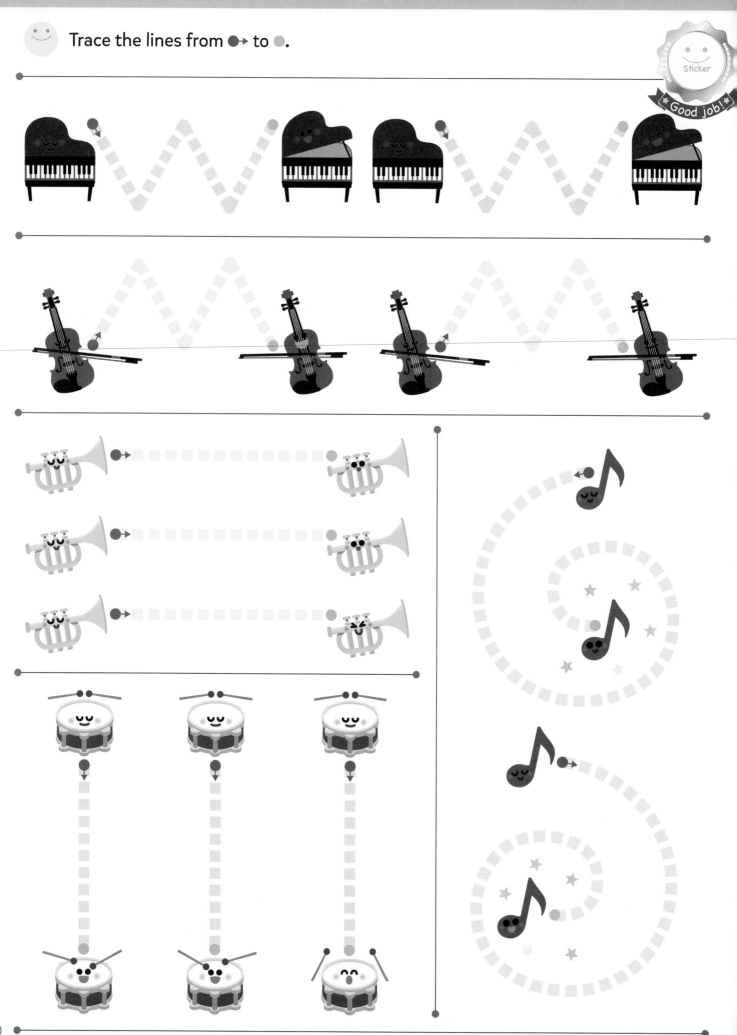

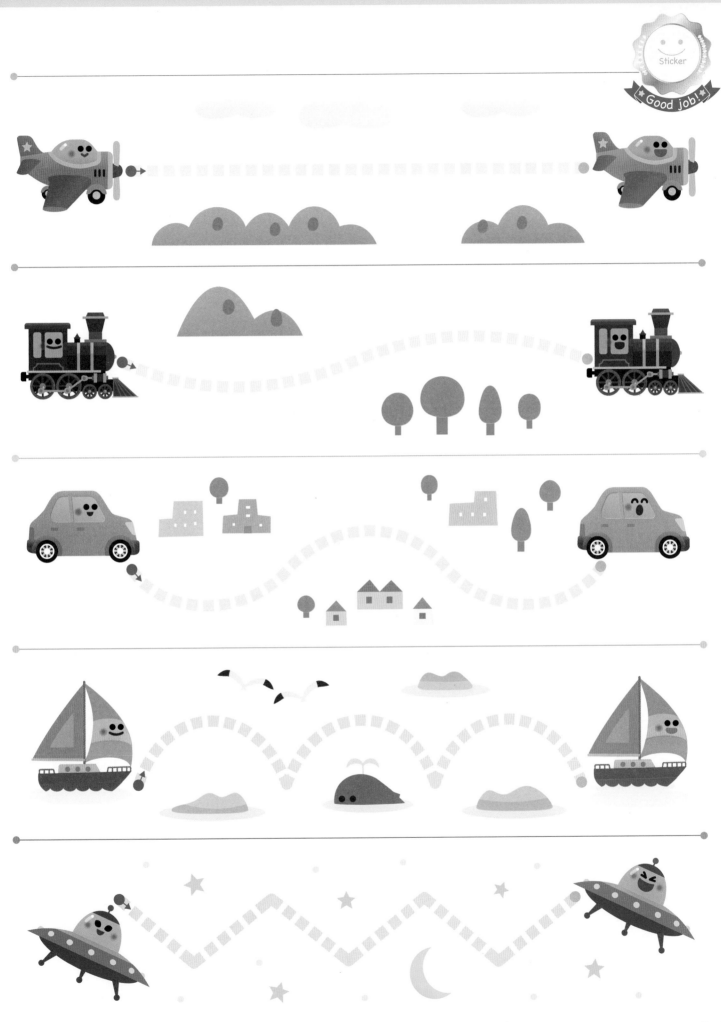

To Parents: The letter A is one of the trickiest letters to write. Encourage your child to focus on the dot at the top of the A. Both lines that go downward need to touch that dot. Then, draw a line across, connecting both sides like a bridge.

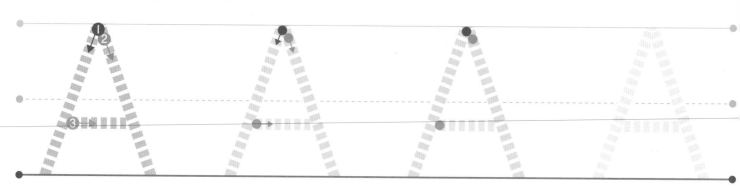

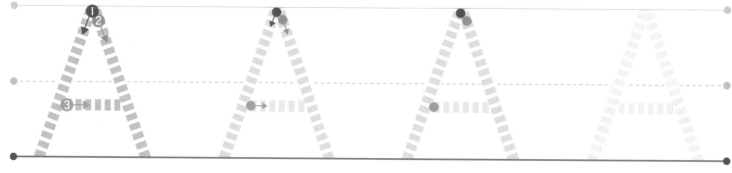

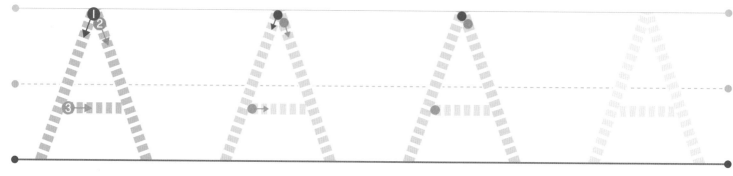

alligator    ant    apple    airplane

a a a a a

a a a a a

a a a a a

alligator

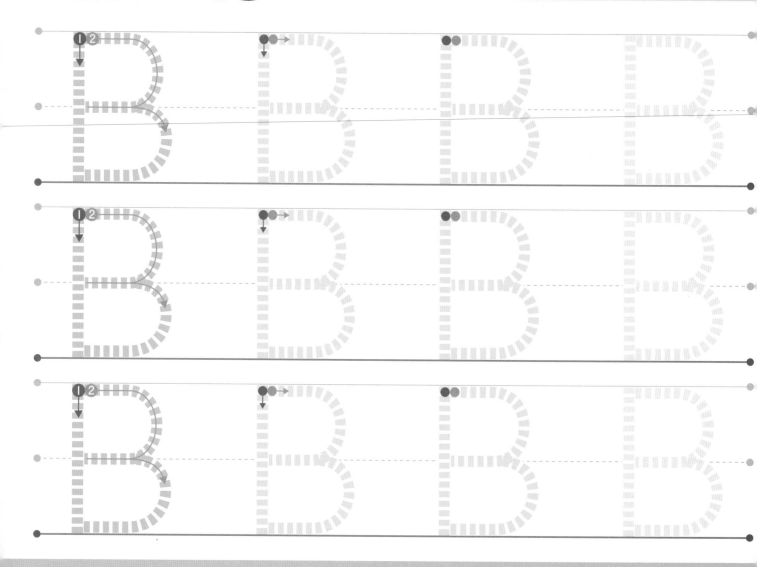

bear    bee   banana    ball

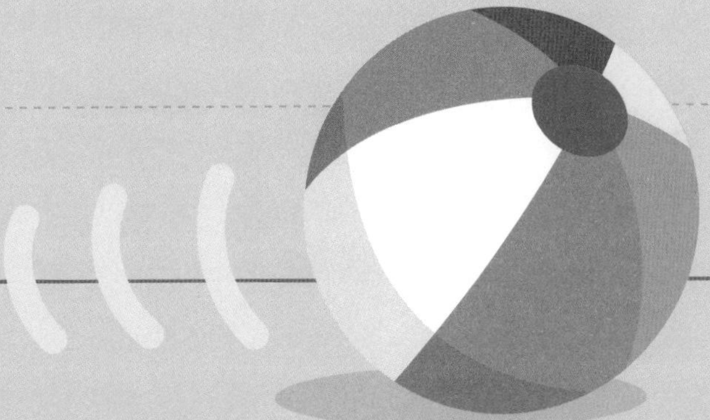

b b b b b

b b b b b

b b b b b

ball

Sticker

Good job!

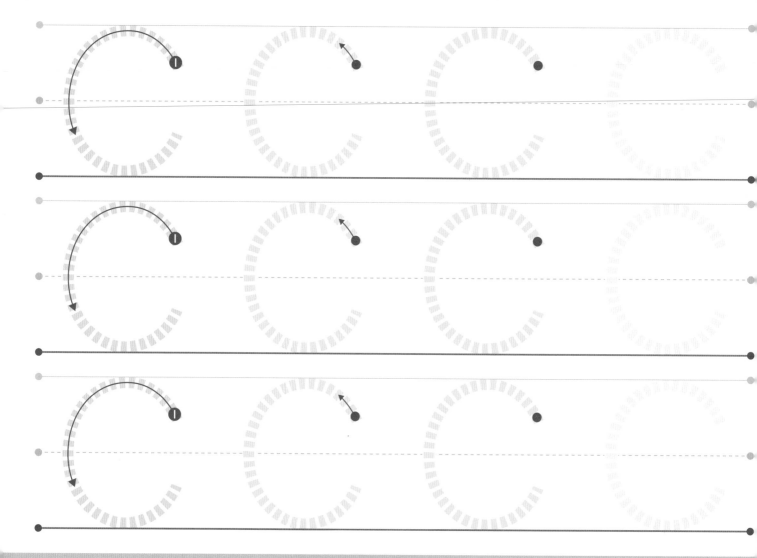

cat   cake   carrot   car

carrot

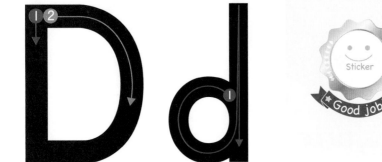

D d

Sticker

Good job!

To Parents: The letter D is made with two strokes—a straight line and a loop that starts at the top of the straight line and goes to the bottom of the straight line. Ask your child to compare how the strokes for uppercase B and uppercase D are similar and different.

dog

dog   **d**uck   **d**oughnut   **d**rum

duck

E e

Sticker

Good job!

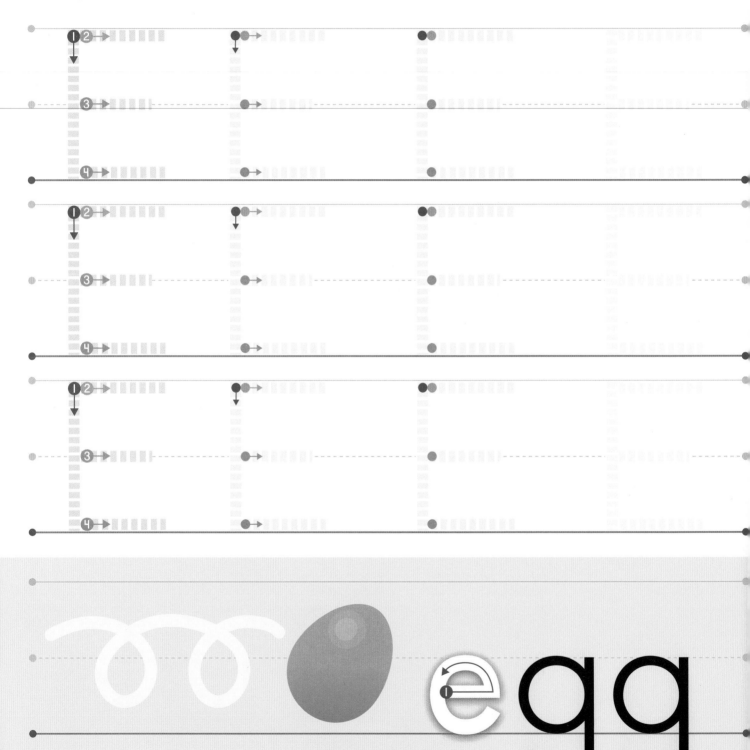

egg

20

elephant   ear   egg   Earth

elephant

F f

Sticker

Good job!

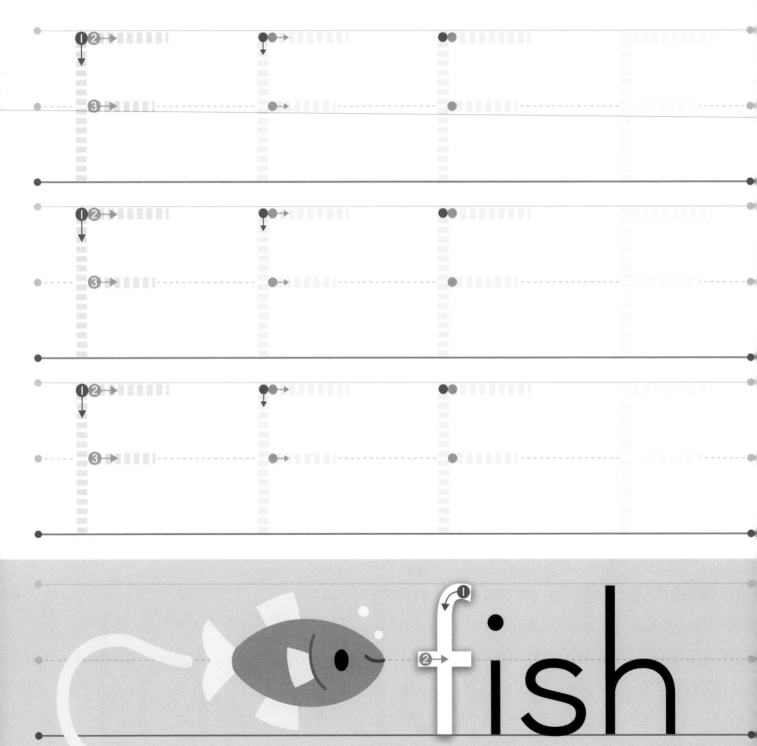

fish

fish   flower   frog   fire engine

frog

G g

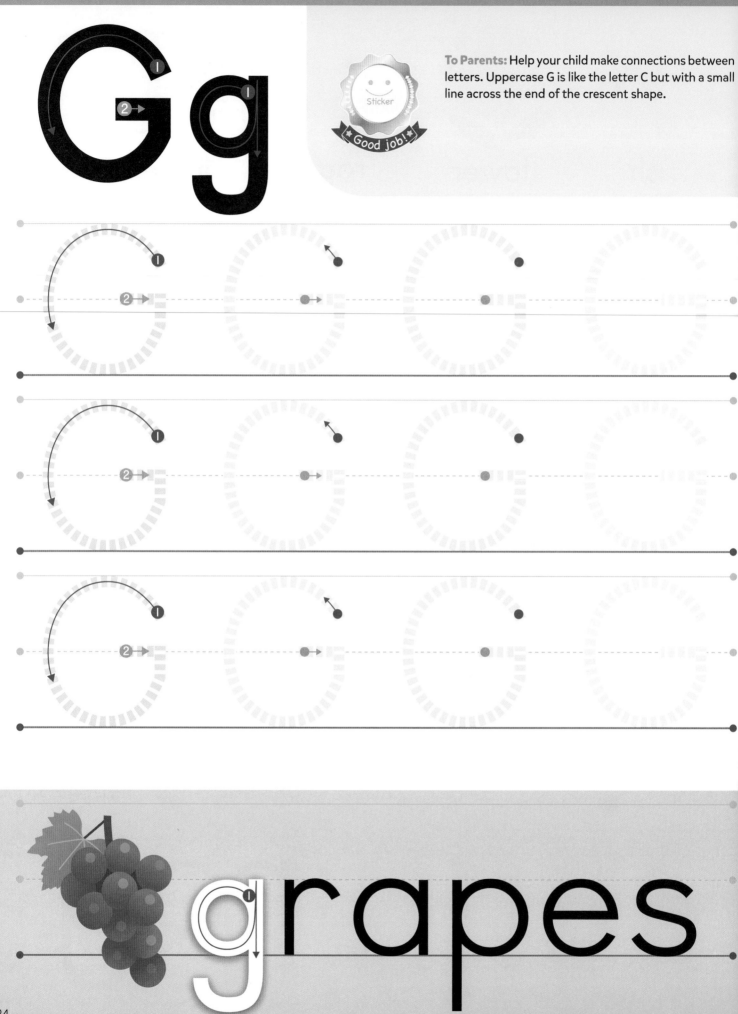

To Parents: Help your child make connections between letters. Uppercase G is like the letter C but with a small line across the end of the crescent shape.

Sticker

Good job!

grapes

24

giraffe

grapes

glasses

guitar

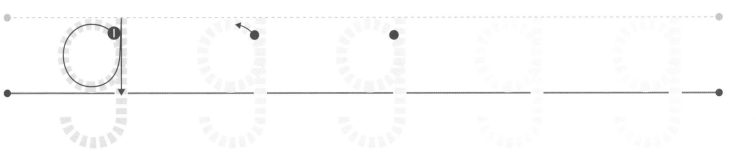

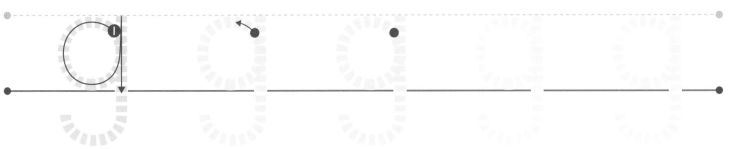

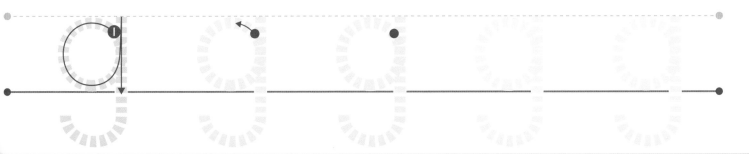

guitar

Hh

To Parents: Some children are very nervous to begin writing. Help ease their anxiety by showing them how to write the letter first. Then, ask them to trace the letter you have written.

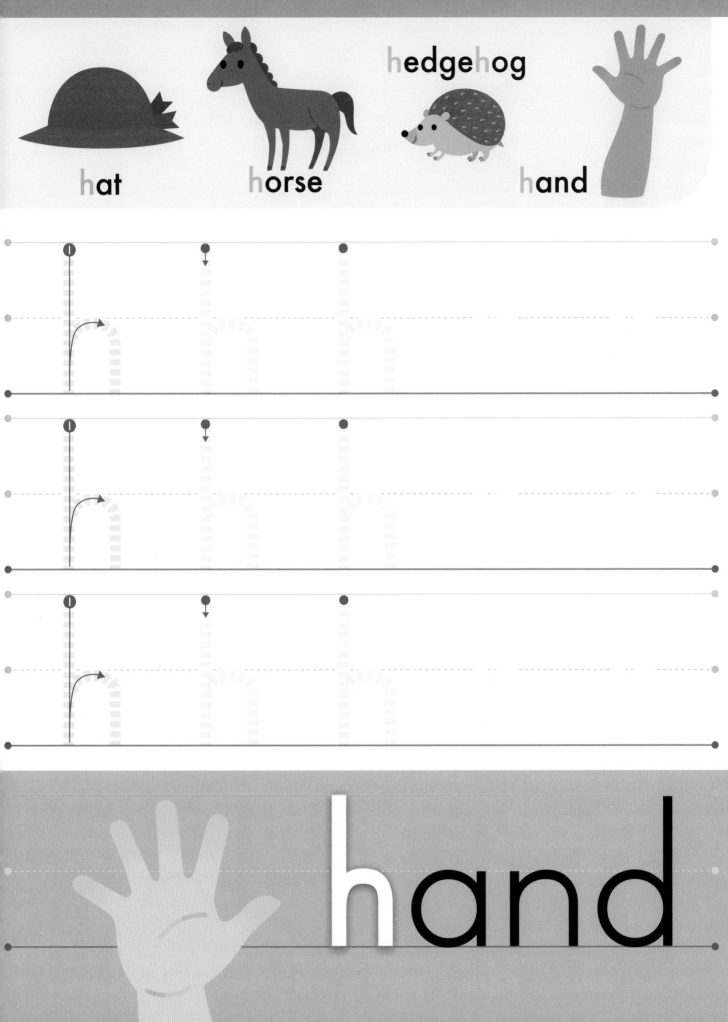

h at

h orse

h edge h og

h and

hand

I i

Sticker

★ Good job! ★

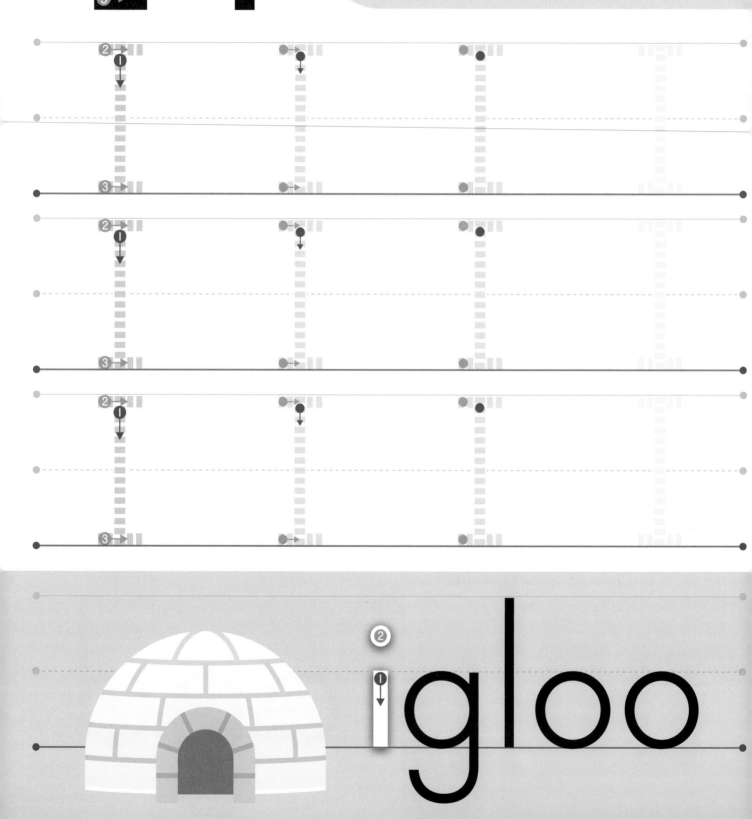

igloo

28

island   iguana   igloo   ice cream

i   i   i

i   i   i

i   i   i

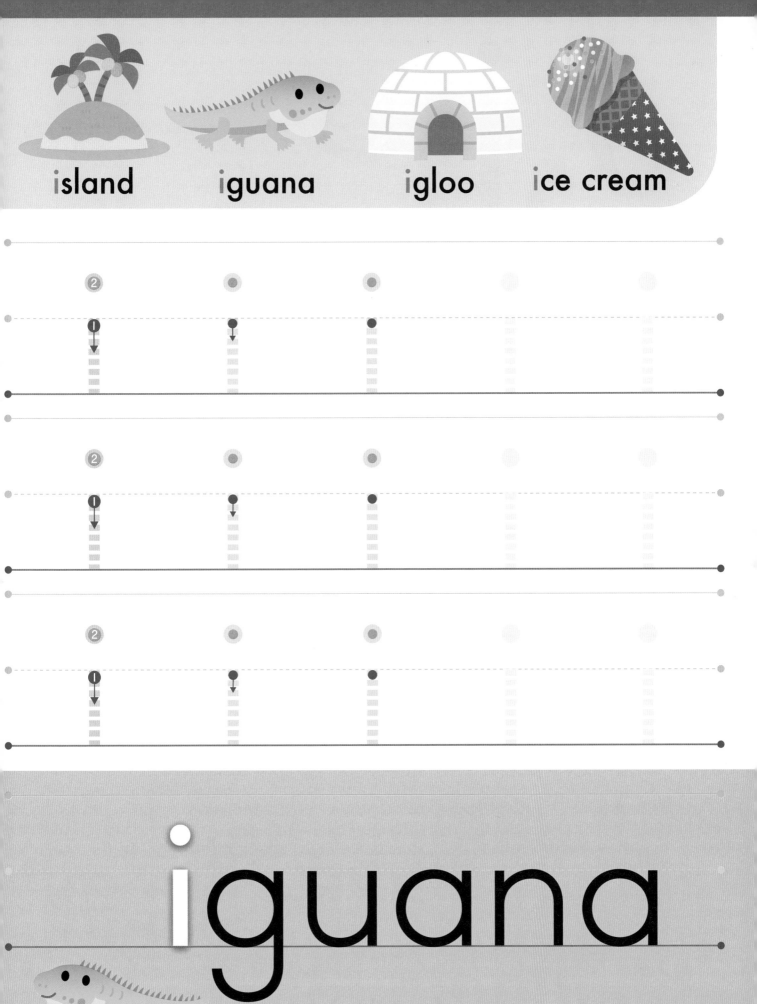

iguana

J j

Sticker

★ Good job! ★

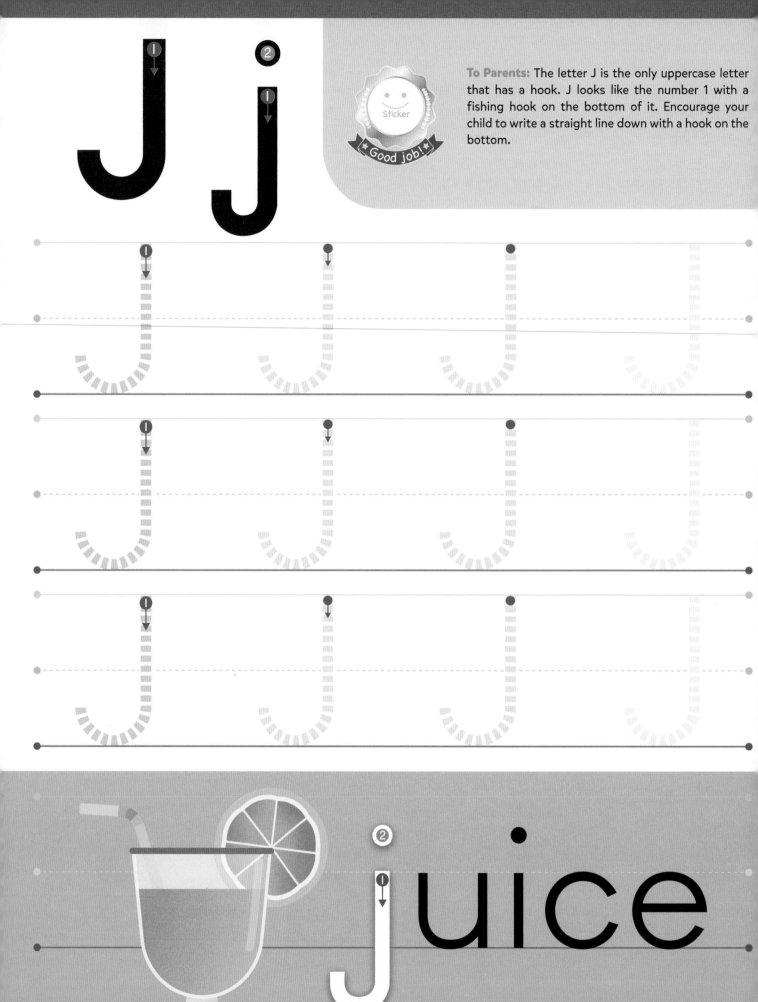

juice

30

juice   jellyfish   jam   jet

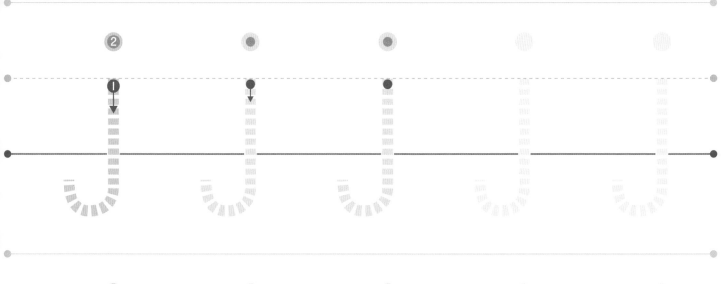

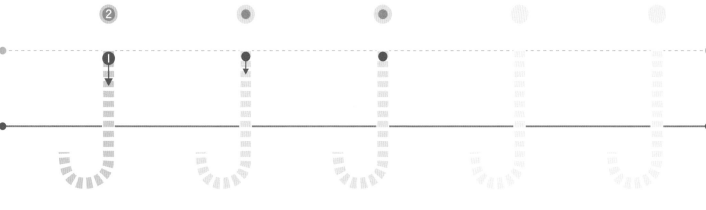

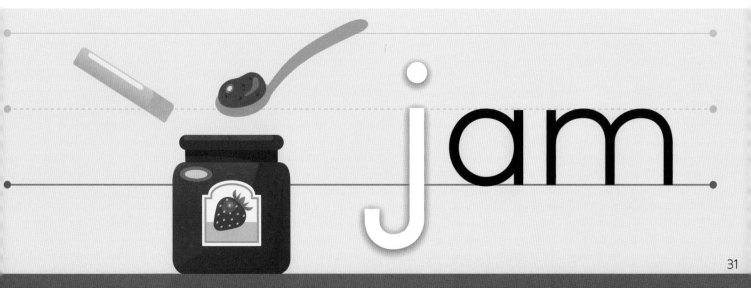

jam

To Parents: The letter K is a very difficult letter for children to learn to write. Encourage your child to make sure that both diagonal lines meet up at the center of the straight line of the K. The diagonal line at the bottom "kicks" out.

Sticker

★ Good job! ★

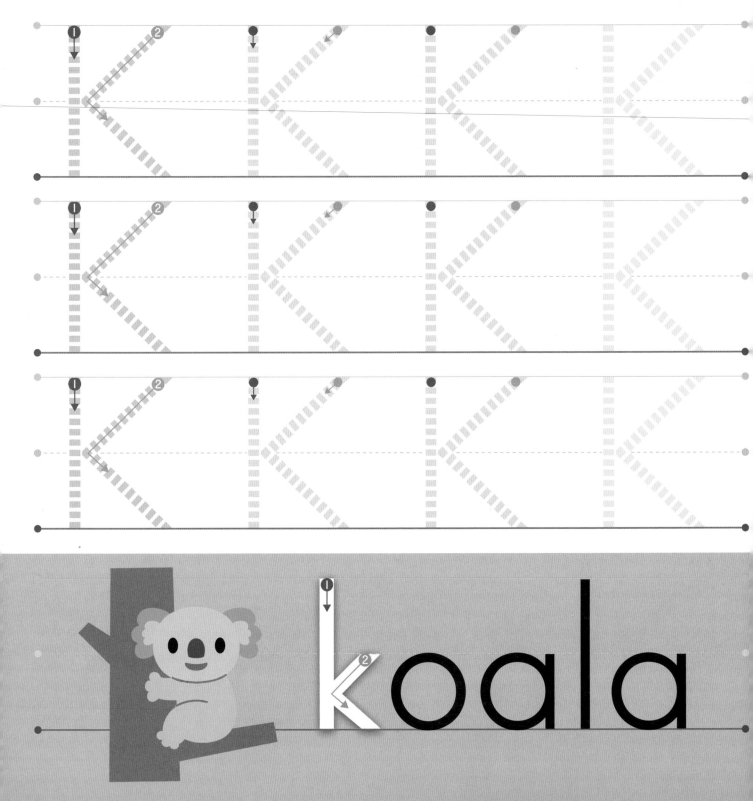

koala

32

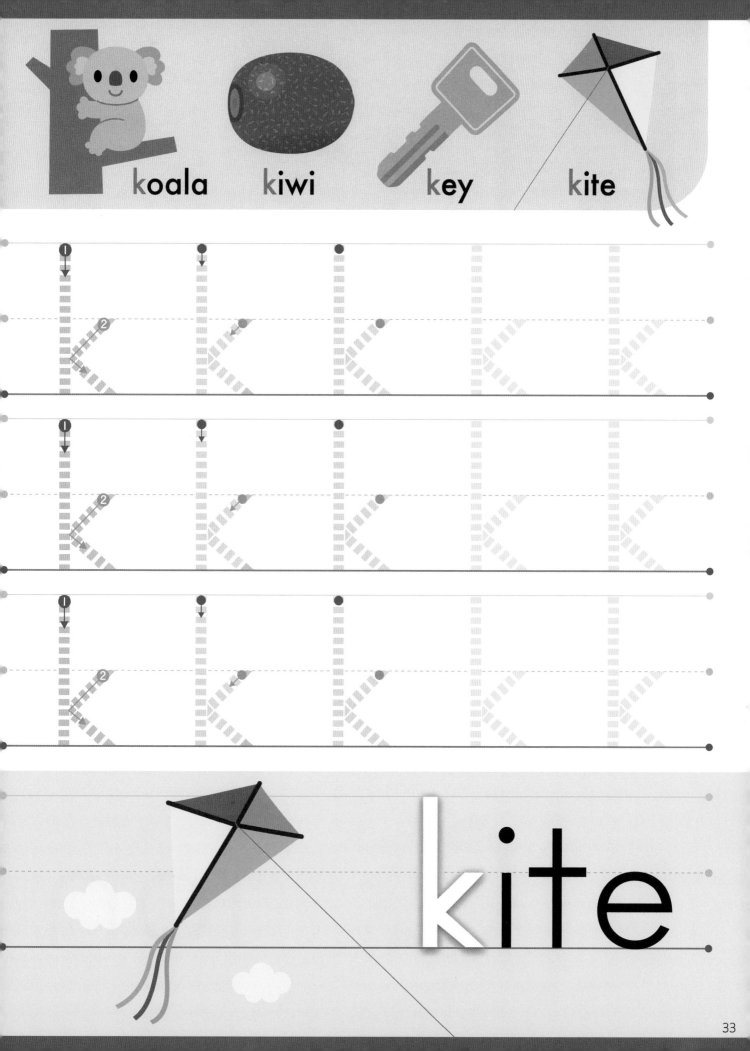

koala   kiwi   key   kite

kite

L l

Sticker

Good job!

lion

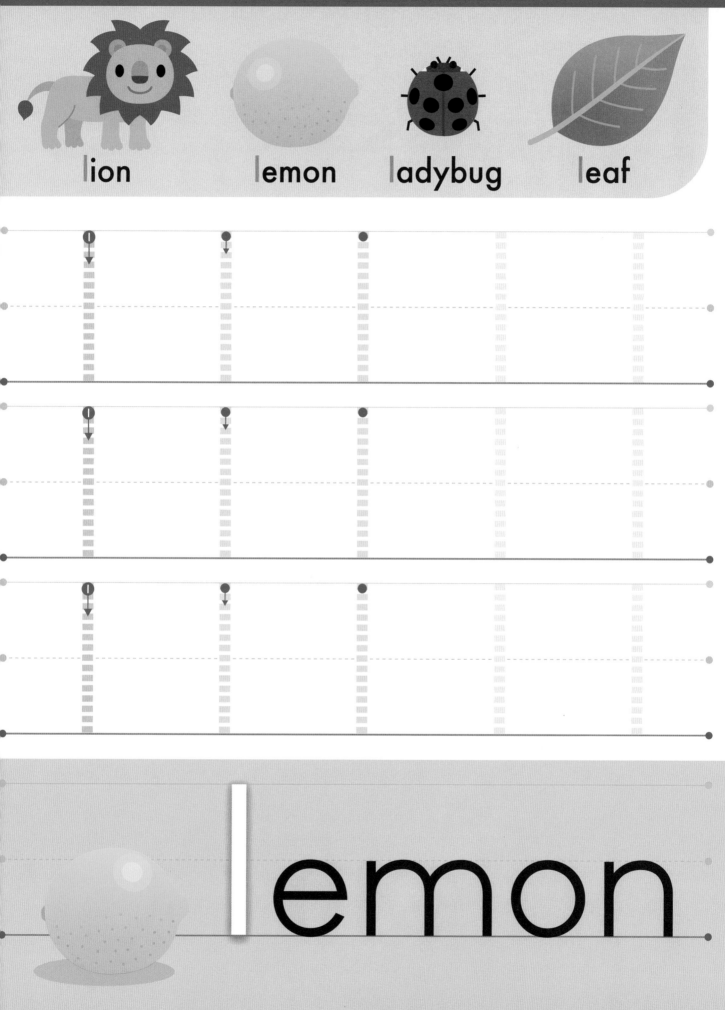

lion   lemon   ladybug   leaf

lemon

M m

To Parents: Point out that uppercase M looks like pointed mountains, while lowercase m looks like small, rounded hills. Give your child a mantra to say as they make each letter. This will help them remember the strokes. "Down, down, up, down" could be their mantra for uppercase M.

monkey

moon monkey mouse milk

m m m

m m m

m m m

mouse

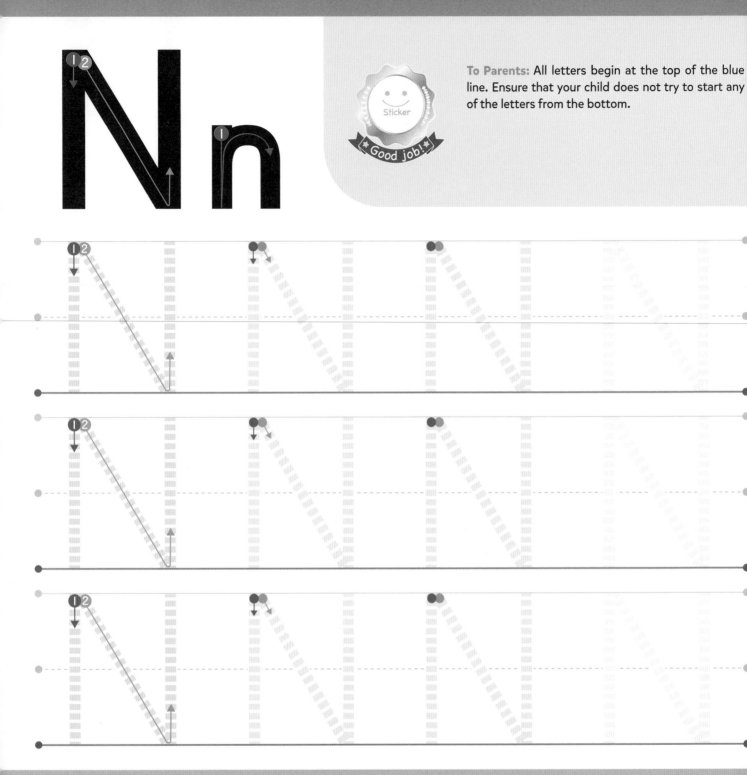

Good job!

Sticker

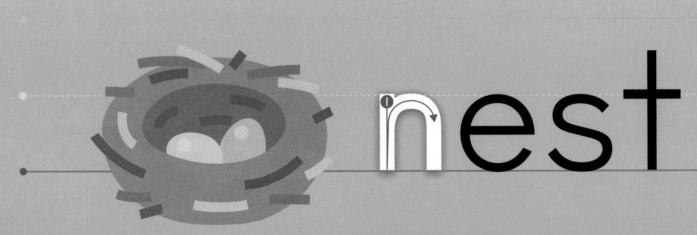

nest

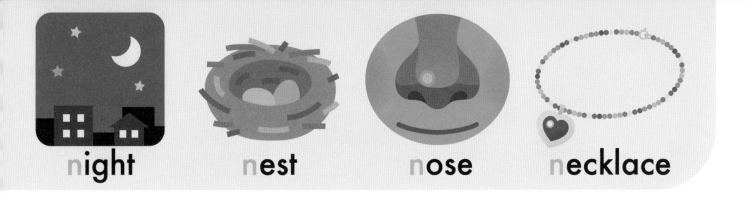

night   **nest**   **nose**   **necklace**

necklace

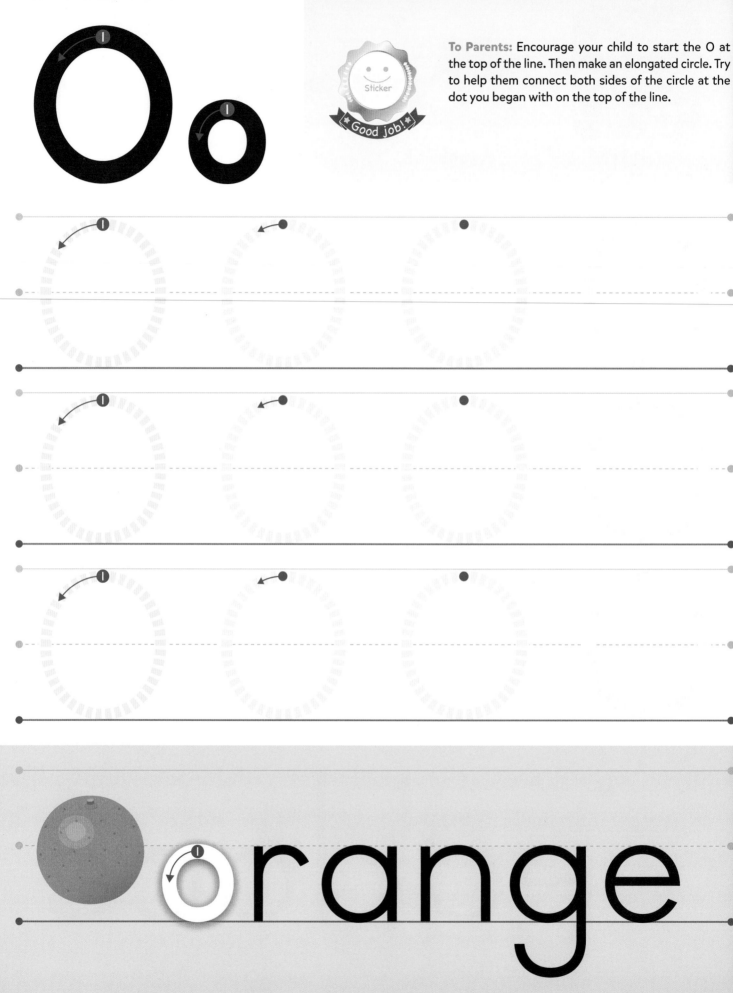

To Parents: Encourage your child to start the O at the top of the line. Then make an elongated circle. Try to help them connect both sides of the circle at the dot you began with on the top of the line.

Sticker

Good job!

orange

orange   octopus   onion   owl

o c t o p u s

P p

To Parents: The letter P is exactly like the first two strokes of the letter B—say, "straight line down, loop to the middle."

Sticker

★ Good job! ★

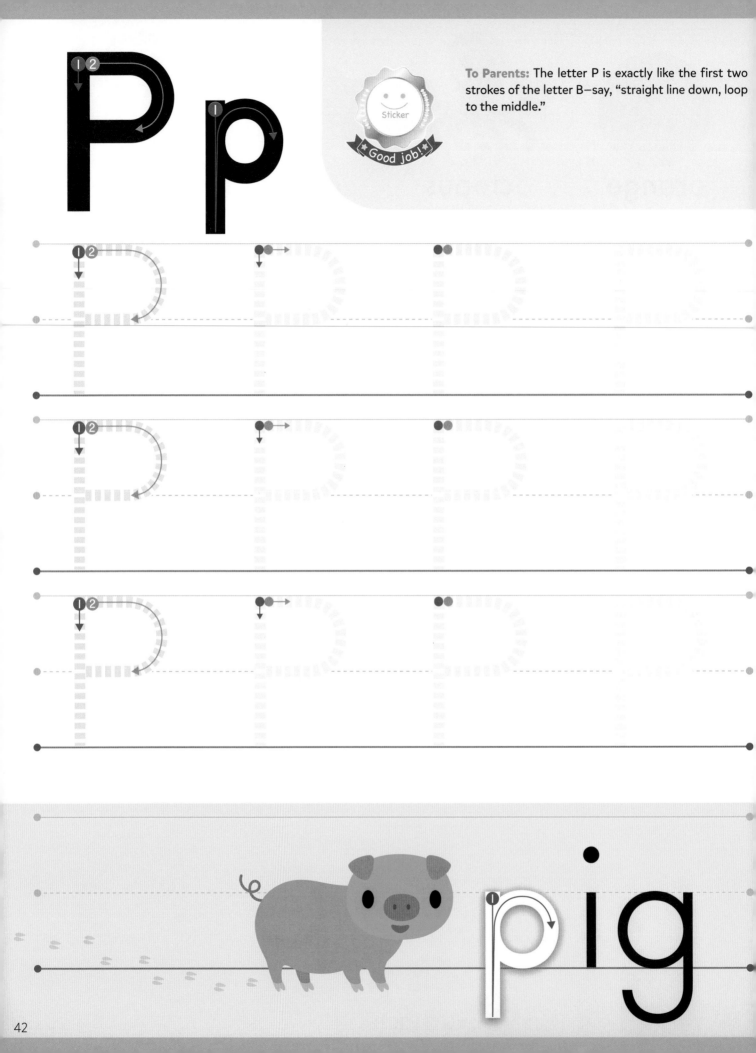

pig

panda pig penguin pear

Q q

Sticker

★ Good job! ★

queen

44

queen   quilt   quail   question

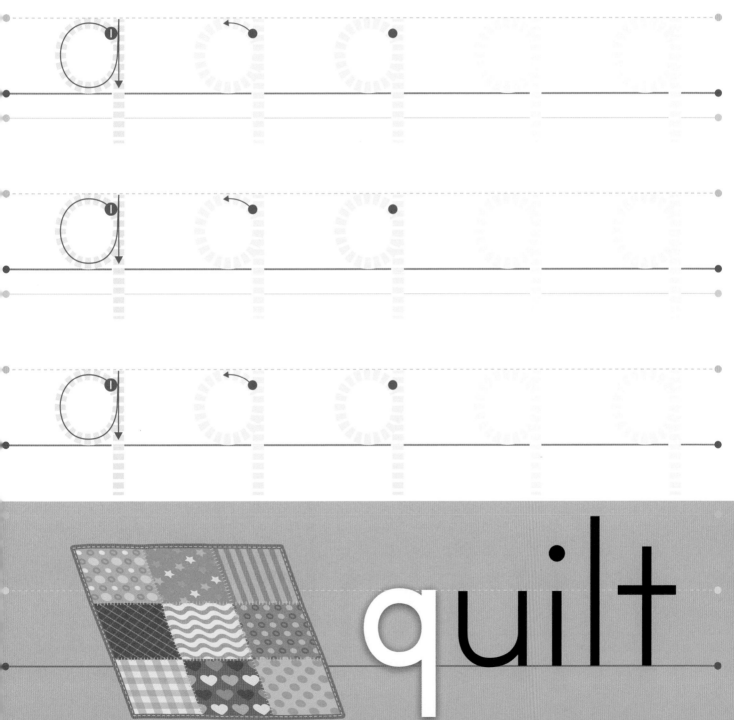

quilt

45

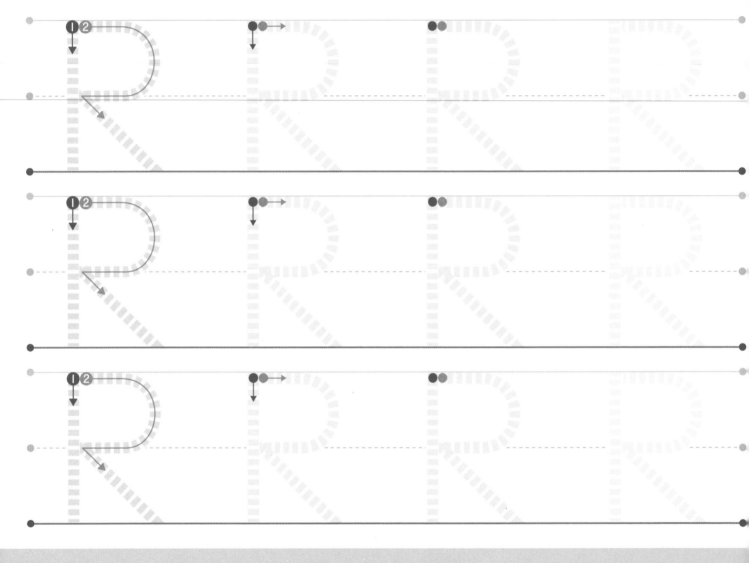

rabbit

rose   rainbow   rabbit   rocket

rose

S s

To Parents: Help your child see that some letters resemble other objects. For example, S looks like a slithering snake! Encourage your child to find the hidden letter C at the top of the S. This will help ensure that they do not reverse the direction of the S.

Sticker

Good job!

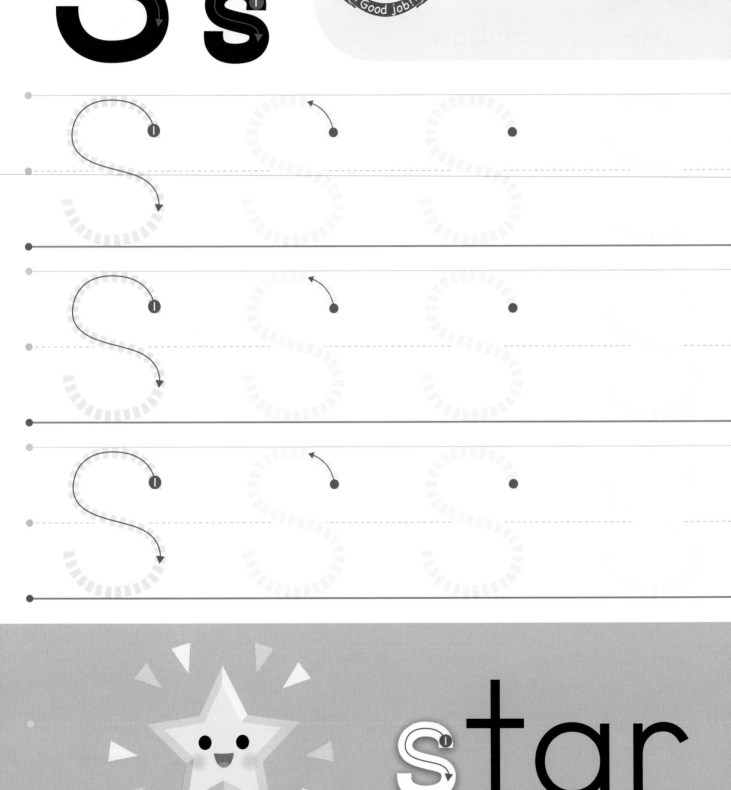

star

48

star   snake   strawberry   sun

snake

To Parents: Uppercase letter T is made the exact same way as uppercase I except it does not have the line at the bottom. Help your child notice the ways that letters are similar and different from one another.

Sticker

★ Good job! ★

tree

50

tiger   tree   turtle   tomato

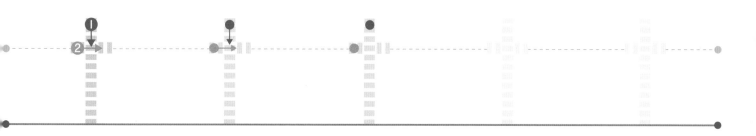

tomato

U u

To Parents: To keep it fun and interesting, play Simon Says: Writing Edition. You might say, "Simon Says find the letter U page and write four Us all by yourself." Making it into a game will help your child develop a positive association with writing.

Sticker

Good job!

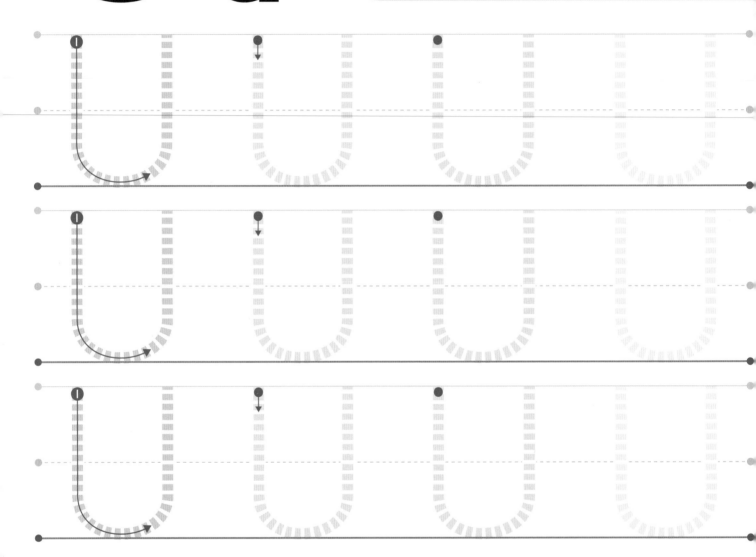

unicorn

52

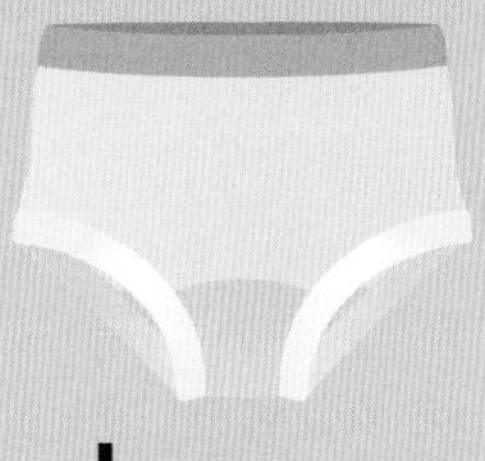

underwear    umbrella    UFO    unicorn

u

u

u

umbrella

V v

To Parents: Teach the letters V and W the same day. Once your child has mastered V, move on to W.

Sticker

Good job!

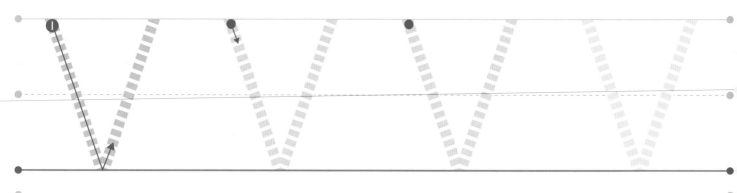

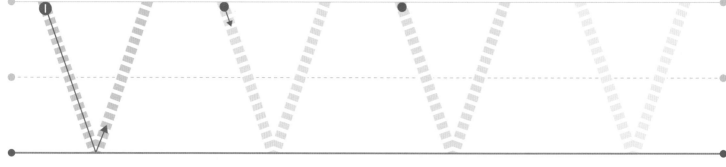

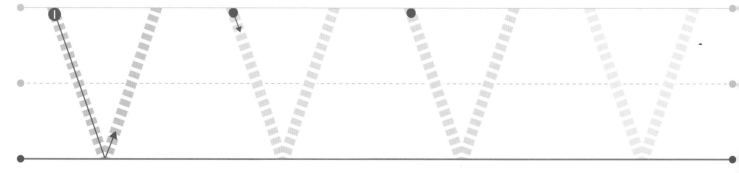

violin

54

vacuum

vegetables

violin

van

v a n

55

Sticker

Good job!

whale

whale    watermelon    wolf   window

W W W W W W W

W W W W W W W

W W W W W W W

wolf

X x

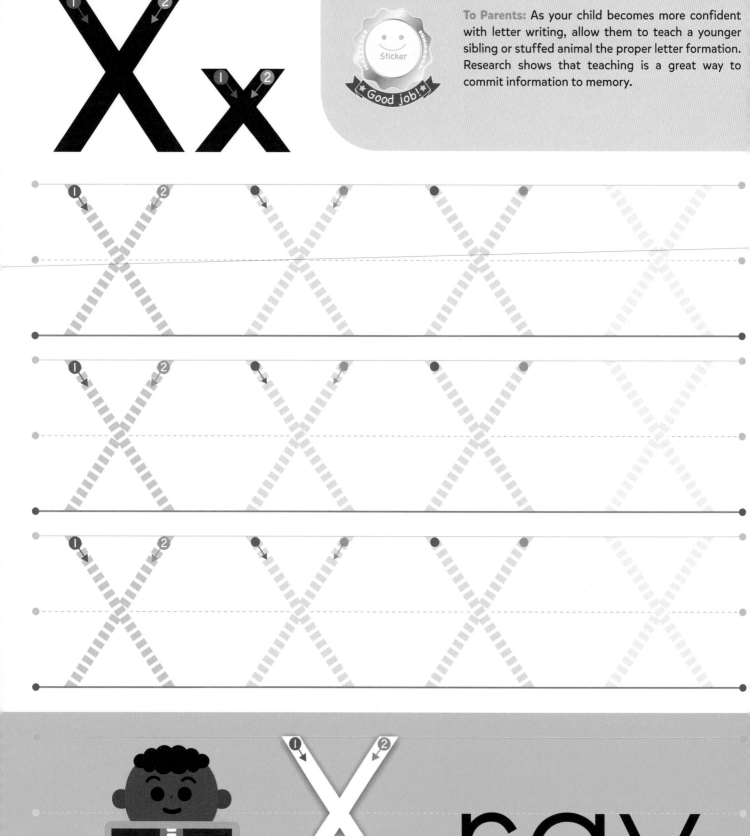

X-ray

X-ray   xylophone   fox   box

box

Y y

To Parents: Have your child notice that the second diagonal line meets the first diagonal line in the middle. Stop where they meet and draw a line all the way down.

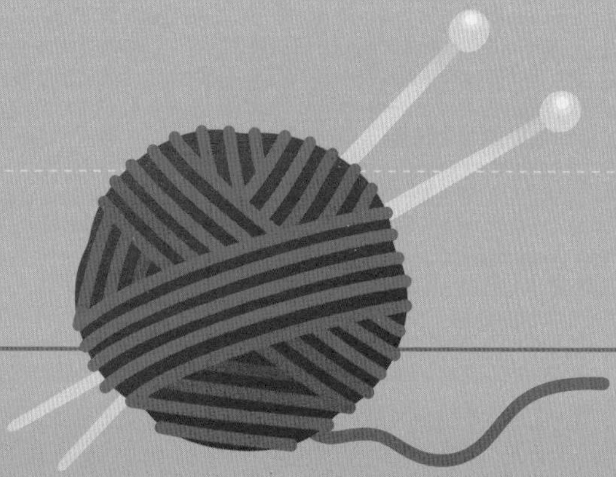

Sticker

Good job!

yarn

60

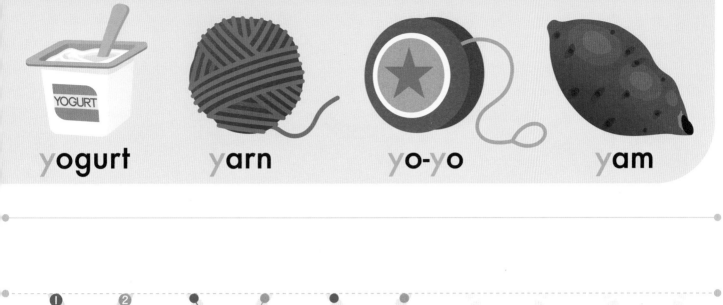

y**ogurt** y**arn** y**o-yo** y**am**

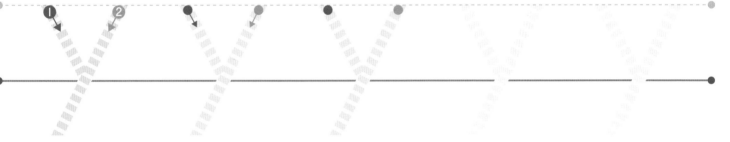

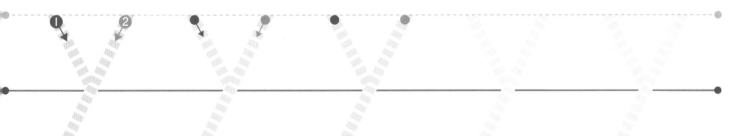

yogurt

To Parents: Children often confuse the letters S and Z as they look similar. However, the two letters face opposite directions. It is helpful to remind your child that Z is a very similar shape to the number 2. It starts with a line across, then a connected diagonal line, and then another line across.

z e b r a

zoo   zoo

zebra 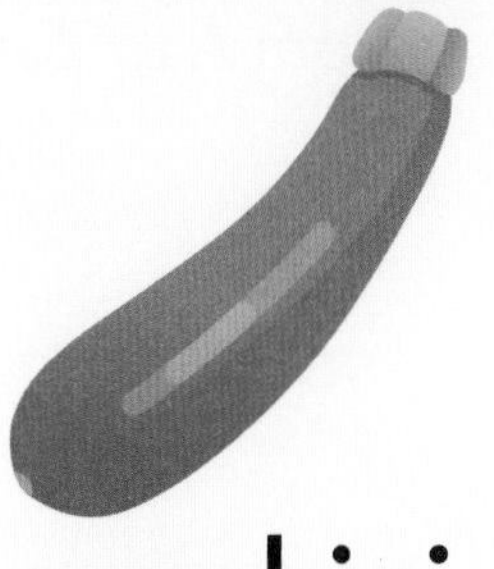   zucchini 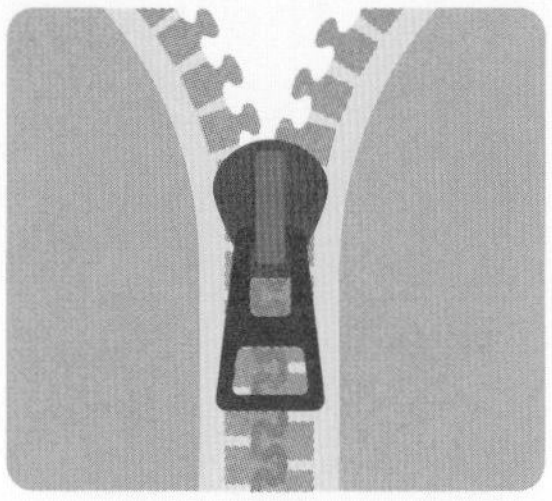   zipper

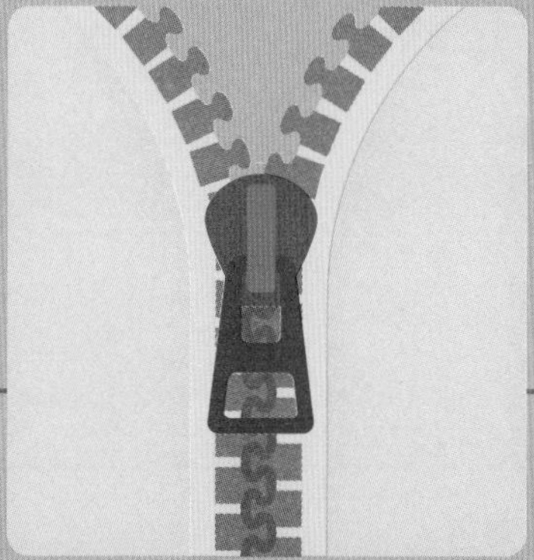

z

z

z

zipper

☺ Trace the letters again from A to Z. Say the word below each letter.

apple   bear   cat

dog   elephant   fish

giraffe   hat   ice cream

jet   koala   lion

monkey   necklace   octopus

Sticker

Good job!

Pp Qq Rr

penguin   queen   rabbit

Ss Tt Uu

strawberry   tree   umbrella

Vv Ww Xx

violin   whale   X-ray

Yy Zz

yo-yo   zebra

To Parents: Encourage your child to trace with a crayon or pencil. If they have difficulty using the crayon independently, have them trace with their finger first.

Sticker

Good job!

one

Write the number and the word. Then, count the objects.

one

2

To Parents: After drawing a curve, have your child stop the pencil once and draw a horizontal line.

Sticker

Good job!

two

67

3

To Parents: Show your child the three flowers on the page. Emphasize that the number 3 represents three objects—in this case, three flowers.

Sticker

★ Good job! ★

three

Write the number and the word. Then, count the objects.

3 three

4

four

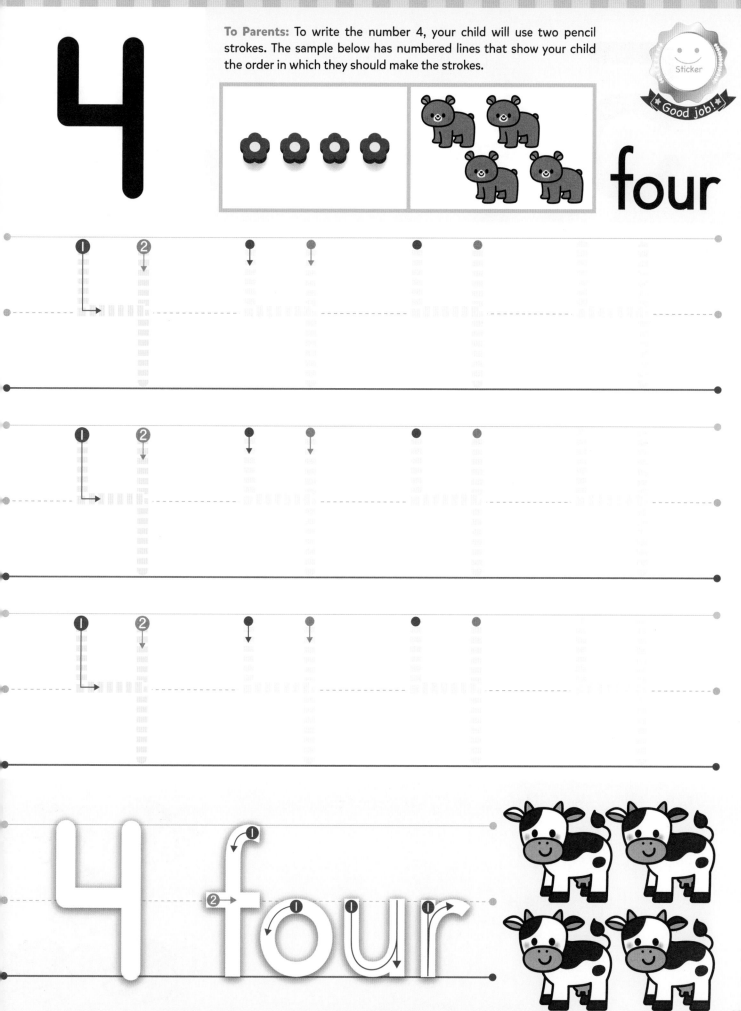

5

Sticker

Good job!

five

Write the number and the word. Then, count the objects.

5 five

6

To Parents: If your child has difficulty writing the number 6, practice drawing the spirals on page 10.

Sticker

Good job!

six

71

7

To Parents: Ask your child to say the number aloud as they trace it with a crayon or pencil.

Sticker

Good job!

seven

Write the number and the word. Then, count the objects.

7seven

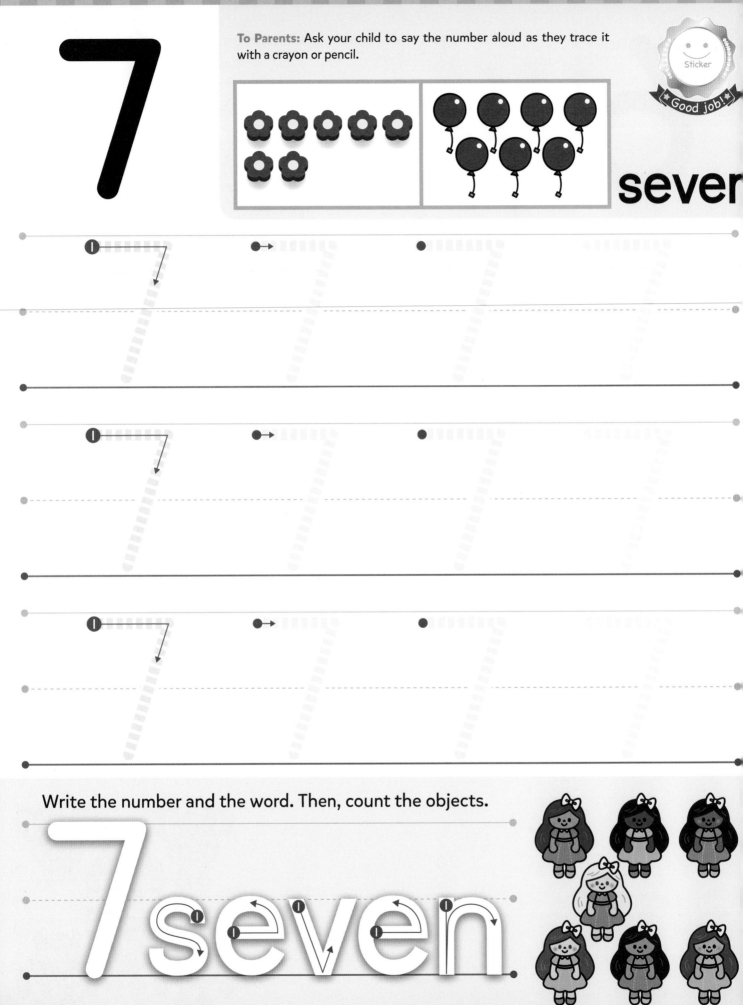

72

8

To Parents: When a child counts several objects, they may lose track. Your child can color, circle, or draw a line through the objects in order to visually recognize what has and hasn't been counted.

Sticker

Good job!

eight

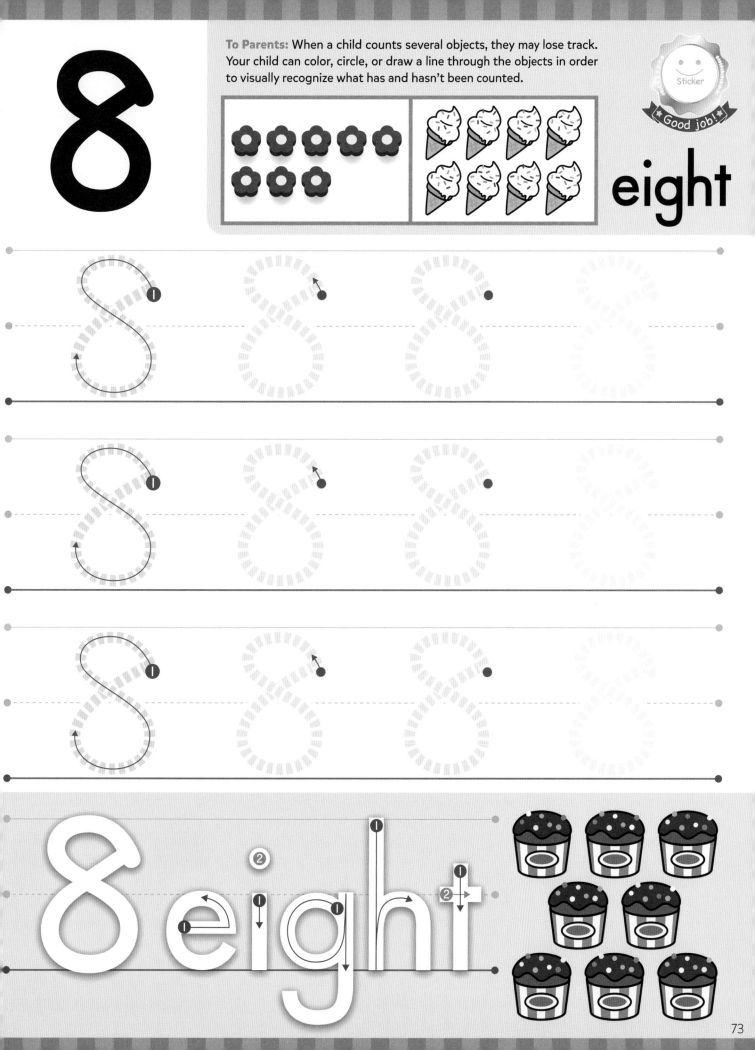

73

q

To Parents: When your child counts objects, make sure they point to each one with their finger. Try placing nine objects on the table and count them together.

Sticker

Good job!

nine

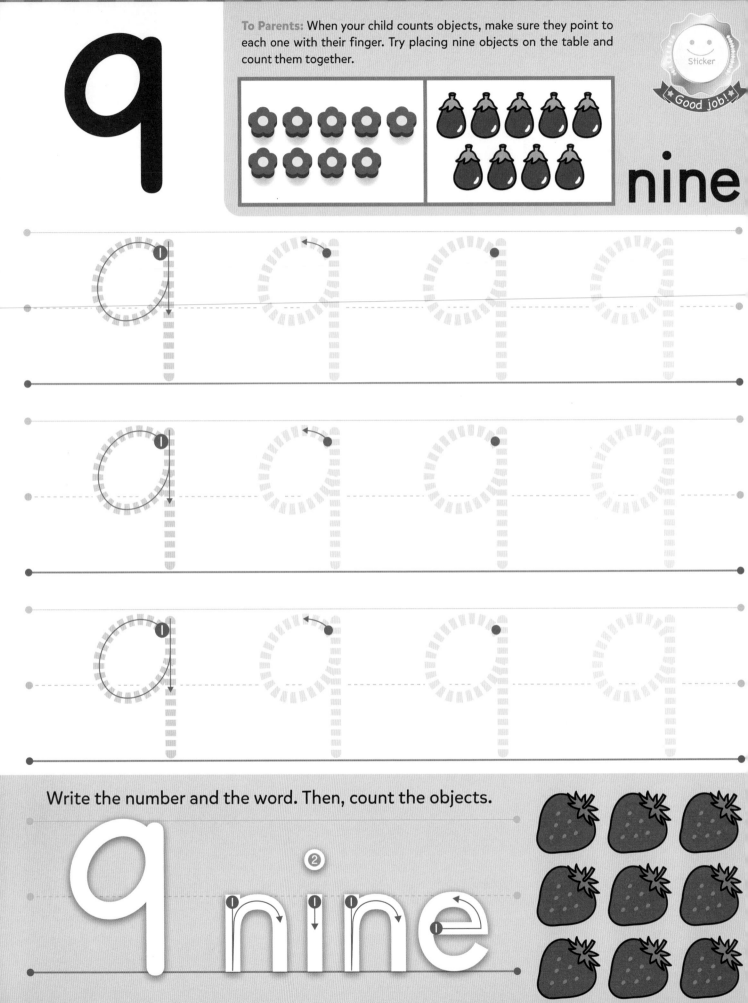

Write the number and the word. Then, count the objects.

q nine

10

To Parents: If your child has difficulty writing the number 0, practice drawing the circles on page 9.

Sticker

Good job!

ten

10 ten

75

Draw a line to connect each number with the same number of flowers. Then, connect each flower grouping with the same number of objects.

example

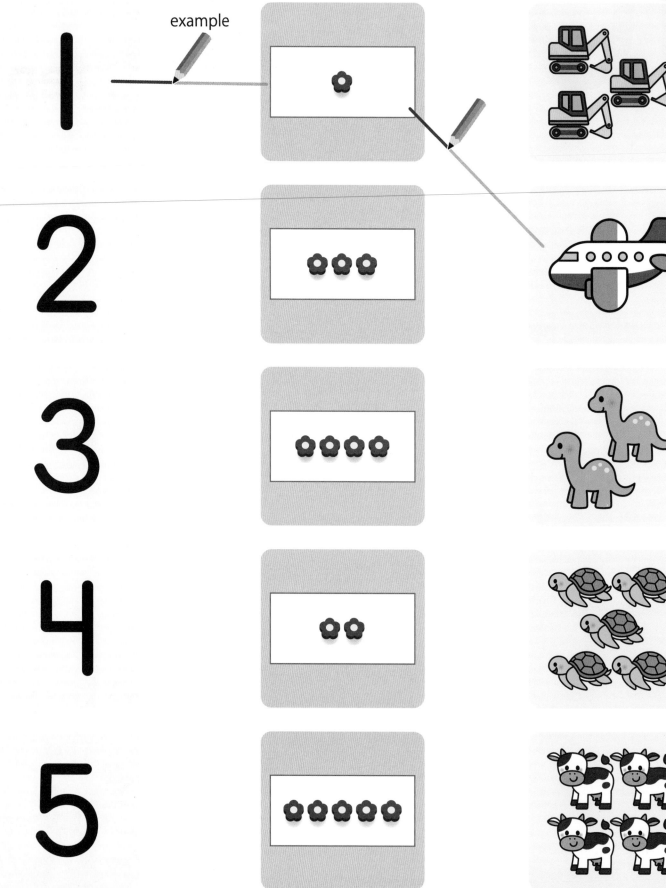

6

7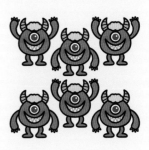

8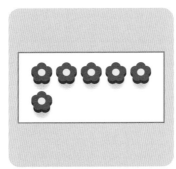

9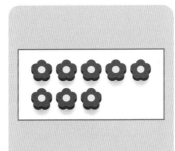

10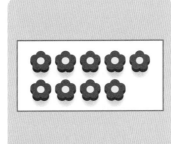

Say the numbers in order from 1 to 10, then trace the numbers below.

1 → 2 → 3 → 4 → 5 → 6 → 7 → 8 → 9 → 10

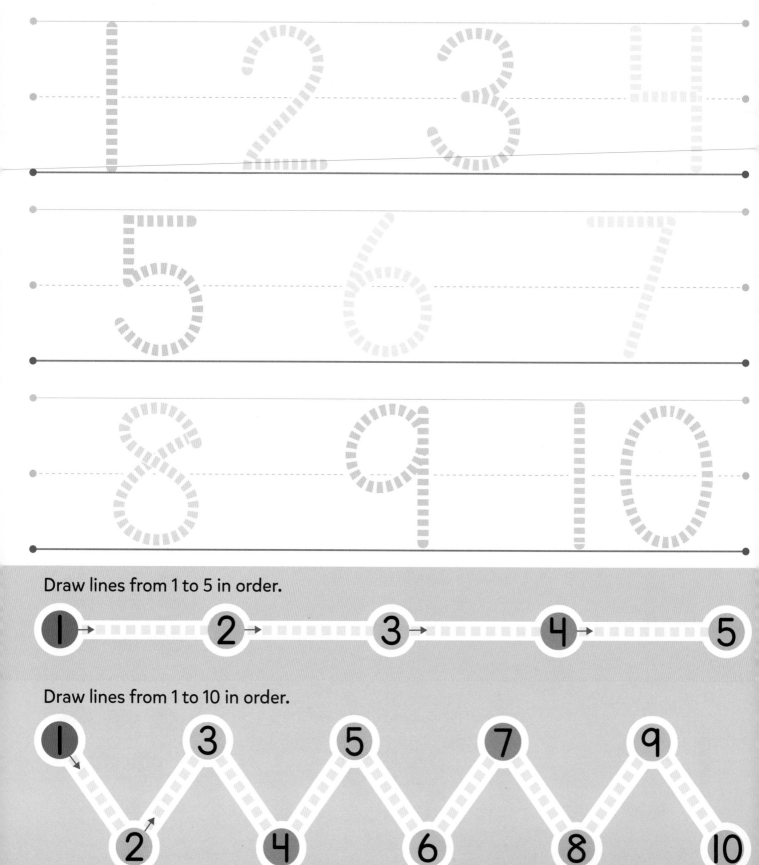

Draw lines from 1 to 5 in order.

Draw lines from 1 to 10 in order.

Draw a line from 1 to 5.

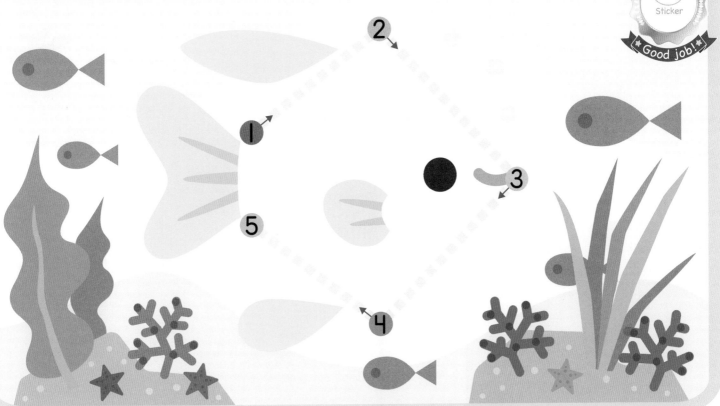

Draw a line from 1 to 10.

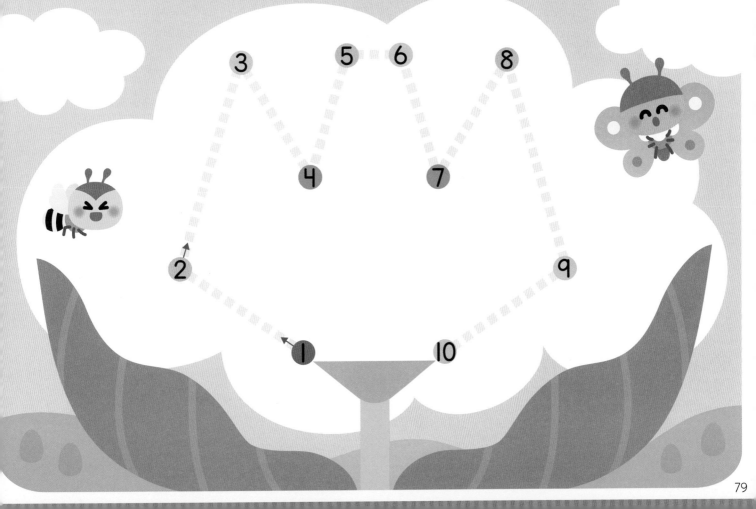

Trace the shapes.

circle

square

triangle

rectangle

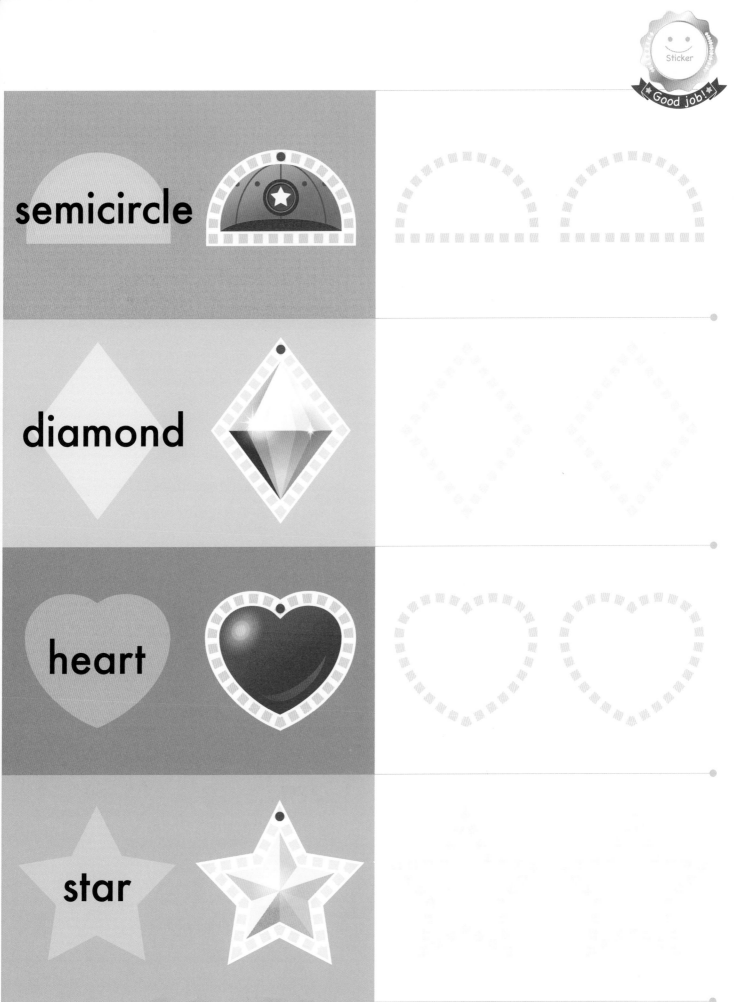

semicircle

diamond

heart

star

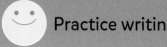 Practice writing your name and age.

First, write your child's name. Then, have your child try to write it.

My name is...

First, write your child's age. Then, have your child try to write it.

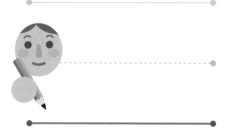

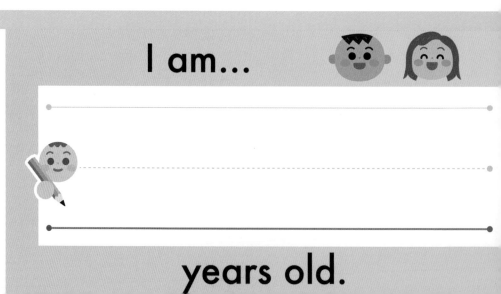

I am...

years old.

Remove this page from the book and tack it on a wall.

apple — A a
bear — B b
cat — C c
dog — D d

elephant — E e
fish — F f
giraffe — G g
hat — H h

ice cream — I i
jet — J j
koala — K k
lion — L l

monkey — M m
necklace — N n
octopus — O o
penguin — P p

queen — Q q
rabbit — R r
strawberry — S s
tree — T t

umbrella — U u
violin — V v
whale — W w
X-ray — X x

yo-yo — Y y
zebra — Z z

ZOO

Remove this page from the book and tack it on a wall.

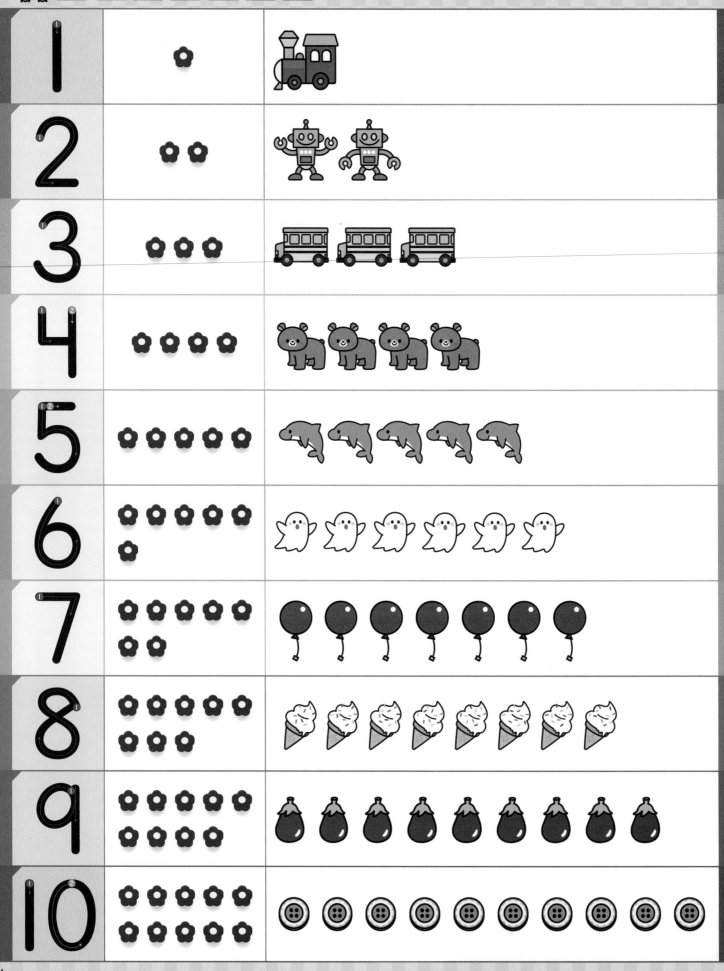